Rain

Focus: Systems

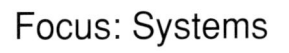

PETER SLOAN &
SHERYL SLOAN

The rain, the wind, and the sun make the weather.

The hot sun shines on water in the sea and rivers and lakes.

The water is warmed by the sun and blown by the wind. When this happens, tiny drops of water are lifted up into the air.

The water drops come
together in the air.
Soon they turn into clouds.

The wind blows the clouds. The clouds become bigger as they are blown together.

The clouds become
heavy with all of the
tiny water drops inside
of them. When they
hit cold air, the clouds
turn into rain.

The rain falls to the
ground and waters
the plants. The rain water
runs into rivers and lakes.
Then the hot sun makes
it happen again.